Extraordinary Praise for

FOR MATURE AUDIENCES ONLY

For Mature Audiences Only is Truthful, Transparent, and Transformative. As in its suggestive title, this offering drives us down the backstretch of truth street and the dark lit alleys of uncomfortable human conflicts in the real 21st century church. In compelling detail, Stephen Hamilton compares and contrasts, revealing self-examination of his burning desire to Shepherd verses the resolve in juggling the reality and actual heat that comes with suddenly being a leader, challenged to lead by example, as a true believer and follower of Christ simultaneously. As in the words of Paul, if the eyes of your understanding are weak, you're challenged to become strong. I cherish the honesty, spirit, and life of Pastor Hamilton in this book. It is ageless and anointed. The question is, will you have Milk or Meat? The takeaway is Grow Big or Go Home!

—**Elder Angela Winbush**
Recording Artist, Songwriter, Producer

For Mature Audiences Only is delightful, helpful, and necessary for a busy person's life. We are in a unique time where God's Word is paramount. Many are preaching and teaching and yet we still struggle with putting God's Word to work. We know that God's word is alive, and Bishop's style of teaching, preaching, and now writing reflects God's intentions of showing love, having compassion, being direct, and having a right now ready to be put to work upon hearing approach.

i

This book is perfect for the mature, solid meat, soldiers for Christ to keep us on track, and I'm more than confident it will help and bless the ones on milk who are seeking specific directions on how to mature in the Body of Christ. God did it again through you! Boom! Breakthrough!

—**Shondrella Avery**
Actor/Producer

I am in awe at the revelation and assignment that was given to Bishop Hamilton that will "help" and "mature" any individual that is willing to succumb to change. We, as pastors and kingdom cohorts, have been trying to find the answer to the diversity of challenges that we all face as leaders in the reality of speaking to this generation and finding a more excellent way to compartmentalize and bridge all cultural proclivities together in order to produce an effective body. Maturity is a word that many people will either run from or tackle with a fresh perspective. I was encouraged, motivated, enlightened, and informed at what this man of God provided for us in the pages of this book.

This is a must-read book for your evolution to Spiritual Maturity, it is one of those manuscripts that will provoke conversation within the walls of ministry. There is apparently a certain subset of believers who have maturity figured out, and the rest of us, are daily trying to pray and seek God for intentional instructions. Religion has taught us misconceptions on what spiritual maturity is, when it happens, where it begins, when it is stunted, and what the true signs of the maturity and immaturity are. I encourage you to read and apply the applications that are given in this book; your questions will be answered.

Thank you, Steve, for providing us your experiences and God inspired revelations to reset us, so that we may obtain the blessings of God.

—Pastor Clinton House
Mountaintop Faith Ministries
Clinton House Ministries

Bishop Stephen Hamilton's *For Mature Audiences Only* is an ingenious literary gift. It takes a unique view at life through the lenses of the Holy Scriptures. It challenges all of us to take responsibility for our spiritual maturation. He accomplishes the tremendous task of joining biblical principles to current cultural issues. *For Mature Audiences Only* is timeless and transcendent.

—Bishop R.C. Blakes
Family of Churches Fellowship International

FOR MATURE AUDIENCES

AUDIENCES

Only

FOR
MATURE
AUDIENCES
Only

Manifesting God's Divine Will
for Your Life Through Spiritual Maturity

STEPHEN HAMILTON

COOKE HOUSE
PUBLISHING
WINSTON-SALEM

FOR MATURE AUDIENCES ONLY: MANIFESTING GOD'S DIVINE WILL FOR YOUR LIFE THROUGH SPIRITUAL MATURITY

Soft cover ISBN: 978-0-9988313-2-9
E-Book ISBN: 978-0-9988313-3-6

Library of Congress Cataloging-in-Publication Data is available upon request

Cooke House Publishing
(a division of Cooke Consulting & Creations, LLC)
2806 Reynolda Road, Suite 274
Winston-Salem, NC 27106
publishing@cookecc.org

This book and all Cooke House Publishing books are available at distributors worldwide.

Printed in the United States of America.- First Edition

Acknowledgements

To my wonderful family, my lovely wife Carla and my incredible children, Angela and Randall! Your love and support inspire me and make me better. I love you.

To my mother Ruby J. Hamilton and my late father Billy R. Hamilton. Thank you for teaching me to love the Lord and His people.

To the members and staff of Spirit and Life Ministries, I'm humbled and honored to be your pastor.

A huge thank you to Givonni Oats and GOOROO Virtual Assist, you made this dream a reality! You are amazing!

Thank you to my publisher Tia Cooke and Cooke House Publishing. Your dedication and commitment to excellence brought the best out of me.

A special thank you to Barbara Wilson for everything you did to make this happen! You're awesome!

Thank you to Carla Hamilton for your input and assistance.

Contents

Foreword

*T*he significant strength of this book is the call to maturity for all the children of God. I have always felt intellectual and spiritual pain when I read the Hebrews writer's comment about Melchizedek: "Of whom we have many things to say, and hard to be uttered, seeing ye are dull of hearing." Obviously, all of us would be privy to the revelatory experience of the Hebrews writer if the members receiving the circular letter were mature enough to handle it. Bishop Stephen Hamilton is declaring that spiritual immaturity is responsible for a lack of revelatory experiences, not only for the immature, but also for all of us who needed them to advance our own spiritual insight.

The immaturity of some becomes a stumbling block for others who chronologically have to follow their generations. This book is dedicated to making sure that we grasp that maturity is the only substratum for sustainable relationships.

The immature must not enter any relationship without having endured situations and circumstances that promote growth.

Patience, in this author's conceptualization of maturity, is not simply a waiting for God to perform, but rather it is the processing of the natural man through carnal to spiritual maturity. Stephen does not leave the immature to plunge into these waters without a lifeguard. The pastor's greatest job is to facilitate this journey into maturity; therefore, Stephen uses a plethora of different personal examples of the encounters he has had as a pastoring lifeguard.

He expostulates how the mature wisdom of a seasoned ministry acts as a catalyst to the end that others under the pastor's watch will experience controlled growth with an understanding. *For Mature Audiences Only* becomes extremely exciting when it expands our cognition to grasp that maturity exhibits itself in a selfless energy.

Our writer thoroughly convinces us that there is no maturity that is self-centered or narcissistic. Maturity seeks the good and advancement of others in its space, whether it is a spouse or a friend. What a great self-assurance growing up evolves into. To revolt from our childish selfishness is to morph into the mature "deny yourself" child of God.

Bishop Hamilton has catapulted us into the intellectual and spiritual heights to seriously seek maturity in all our relationships!

Thank you, Stephen, for this must read.

Bishop Noel Jones
City of Refuge Church
Los Angeles, CA

Introduction

*W*hat did we miss out on? The apostle Paul, believed by many scholars to be the author of the book of Hebrews, wanted to give a deeper understanding to the Hebrew believers comparing the superior priesthood of Jesus Christ to that of the Old Testament priest Melchizedek. Paul said he had "much to say about this, but it is hard to make it clear to you because you no longer try to understand. In fact, though by this time you ought to be teachers, you need someone to teach you the elementary truths of God's word all over again. You need milk, not solid food!" (Hebrews 5:11-12 NIV) Paul wanted to give his audience, the Hebrew believers, encouragement that Jesus is a better, more effective high priest than not only Melchizedek but also the Levitical priesthood. He would go on to expound on it in chapter seven, but he hesitated in chapter five because they were babes still on "milk," not of "full age," and not ready for "solid food" (spiritually mature). We will never know if there was some additional information or profound revelation Paul was unable to share with his audience—and subsequently us as readers of the Word—because they weren't mature enough to receive it.

The mature believer can receive instruction, information, and correction, and will apply it to their lives and to the benefit of others as well as themselves. They will even use trials, challenges, mistakes, and failures, in addition to successes, as opportunities for growth and development. When you are dealing with an immature believer, you may find yourself having to go over the same information again and again, not because it is too difficult, but because of a lack of focus, desire, or willingness to receive instruction. In many cases, you can measure an individual's level of maturity by how they react when things do not go their way or if they do not get what they want. If they begin to pout, throw tantrums, or act out, that is a sign that you are dealing with someone who lacks maturity.

When an individual is spiritually mature, they seem to go through life with a certain level of faith and confidence in God which keeps them steady and composed, even in the middle of difficult or challenging circumstances. They're not exempt from trials and tribulations, but they seem to cope with them differently. They also seem to have a greater sense of direction, purpose, and focus. Moreover, the mature believer is an asset to the local church and to the community they live in. They often become leaders who, like an older brother or sister in a family, can help develop and train those that come behind them.

I began to wonder, *What are we missing out on now because of our immaturity?* Are there deeper revelations and blessings that we've been unable to tap into because we weren't spiritually mature? I've been privileged to serve as a ministry leader for thirty-seven years and as a senior pastor for twenty-seven years. Many of the challenges I've had to overcome was not only my own lack of maturity but also the immaturity of those I was trying to lead; we all had a lot of growing up to do! Very early in my pastorate, I had to face the harsh reality that nothing was going to happen overnight, I had to grow into my role as a pastor, and that the small congregation was watching to see if I could handle my new position.

In the early years, we seemed to have great momentum and there was a level of excitement around our ministry that we'd never experienced before. I began to think we were ready to take the next step and take me off my job as a mailman and move into the role of a full-time pastor! I took the idea to my dad, who was also the church administrator, but much to my surprise, he didn't share my enthusiasm. In fact, he said it was more impressive that I was a working pastor. I learned a valuable lesson from that experience—that both I and my congregation had to mature if we were going to go to the next level. A few short years later, I retired from the U. S. Post Office and went into ministry full-time. What I wanted to happen years before, had been delayed until I had matured, learned to be patient, and realized that everything doesn't happen overnight. The deacons and the board of directors also had some growing to do. They had to learn to trust their young pastor, trust God, and move by faith to finally have a full-time pastor.

Now more than ever, mature, responsible, spiritually-connected individuals are needed, not only in the local church but also in our communities. Sometimes it can seem like there are no grownups in the room, so few seem able to bring order to a chaotic situation, accept responsibility, or provide direction and leadership.

Just as you would not put the key to a Ferrari into the hands of your seventeen-year-old who just received their license, God is not going to drop the keys to the Kingdom on babies. In this time of uncertainty and fear, God is getting a group of people together that are mature, focused, and ready to move forward.

This book issues a challenge to the body of Christ: are we ready to walk in spiritual authority and be a body of believers as Jesus said, "the gates of hell won't prevail against it"? Are we prepared to accept the "keys to the kingdom of heaven" so God can use us to accomplish His will on earth as it is in heaven? Are we ready to launch out into the deep to become fishers of men, sharing our faith and the love of Jesus with the world? If we follow the principles in this book, we will be ready to handle "strong meat" and able to operate on the level God has ordained for us.

Chapter 1

Mature Believers:
By This Time You Ought to Be Teachers

*W*hat happened to us? Why does it seem so hard for us to grow up? Oftentimes, it seems that we are stuck in a vicious cycle of starts and stops, never advancing in our walk with God. How many times have we declared that we were ready to do great things for God only to find ourselves stuck in the same rut, repeating the same mistakes over and over again?

There are many factors that may have an impact on our ability to grow. A few are our environment/upbringing, society, and the Church. All play a role in the development of a child of God.

1. **Environment/Upbringing**: The experiences and people you have been exposed to can have a massive influence on your development. The less exposure we have to the wide variety of things that life has to offer, the less is our ability to develop a much-needed appetite for something more or something greater. This often manifests itself in how we appreciate music, the arts, fine dining, and even fashion. When I was growing up, along with my six siblings, going to a sit-down restaurant was an extremely rare occurrence. It was too expensive for all of us to go. (Even fast food was a treat.) So, my exposure to different types of cuisine was extremely limited until I became an adult and began going to different restaurants and trying and enjoying various dishes, developing a wider palette. I'm glad to have been exposed to something more and have been able to do the same for my children.

    Events and circumstances that are part of our formative years can have a lingering effect on our spiritual, emotional, and psychological development. This lack of maturity can manifest itself later in life when we find ourselves making questionable choices and unwise decisions regarding our relationships, careers, finances, and health. I have dealt with people who seemed to be stuck in a vicious cycle demonstrating the lack of a mature mind. They live their lives in a kind of time capsule, if you will, continuing to date (and in some cases marry) people from that long-lost era of their life. However, we cannot grow if we remain stuck in moments from our past, whether they are positive or negative.

Many of us have experiences from our childhood that have had a lasting impact on us well into adulthood. Some have lost a loved one, or saw their parents split up, others were in an abusive situation, or were told they'd never amount to anything. These negative experiences can affect how we view ourselves and others, dimming our hopes and expectations for the future and keeping us bound to our difficult past. The same can also be true of positive experiences. Some of us really excelled when we were in high school, or when we were kids; we may have been the star athlete, class president, homecoming queen, or most popular. But when we got older and life became more difficult and didn't go the way we expected, we find ourselves stuck in the past, trying to relive our glory days. We must trust God and be strong enough to get up, dust ourselves off, close that chapter of our life, and turn the page to reveal God's "next" for our lives.

It's also beneficial when we are raised in a spiritual home: a place where even as a young child you are taught to love God, how to pray, and to have and develop faith. One of the trends I've seen in recent years is there are more un-churched individuals in our ministry. We must do more teaching on the basic principles that many of us were taught at home as children. It's exciting to see them grow and get fired up and become eager to learn more, once they have developed a healthy appetite for the things of God.

2.   **Society**: As believers, we must be careful of society's role in our development. God's people cannot allow society (the world) to continue to be a somewhat detrimental example that shapes how we think, feel, and behave, nor can it be the main source of our mental, emotional, and spiritual nourishment. Consuming this type of spiritual diet alone will leave a child of God feeling anxious, weak, and defeated due to the amount of negative, carnal, spiritually unhealthy content, and fake news that we entertain.

Social media has been an incredible way for individuals to connect and reconnect with friends and family. It has also been beneficial in allowing us to meet new people and expand our business and ministry outreach. However, it has also become a new source of peer pressure for adults. When we see our friends "living their best lives," seemingly eating at the best restaurants, going on amazing vacations, shopping at the finest stores, and attending awesome events, a feeling of competition and jealousy begins to develop in us. You are not alone; this happens to all of us. Pastors and preachers feel this pressure too. The overwhelming desire to compete and have more followers and get the most 'likes' can leave you frustrated, discouraged, and feeling inadequate based on what is posted on social media. We cannot continue to compare ourselves using this filtered, edited, and oftentimes, distorted reality. Society can influence us in many ways by what we see, hear, and read. We must be careful that we do not consume so much that we allow it to stunt our growth and maturity.

3. **The Church**: We cannot ignore the role the church plays in our development (or lack thereof). The Church's impact on a child of God is huge. If it is a place where its members are free and are energized to develop a personal relationship with God, then that will be a strong, mature church. But if the members are bound and under the control of an insecure leader who lacks vision, they will be malnourished and underprivileged. Sometimes it seems as if some of the people that should encourage our growth and development try their best to discourage and hinder it.

I grew up in an old-fashioned church that was very conservative and espoused traditional values and culture. This was in the seventies and eighties before the Internet and social media. We were only exposed to what our pastor allowed us to be exposed to. We could not visit other churches, especially ones outside of our denomination. This limited exposure created an environment of manipulation, control, and fear. It also stunted our growth and development. We only heard the scriptures taught or preached with a focus on our doctrine, man's tradition, and long-held opinions of the pastor. We felt bound and lived in fear of getting caught breaking any of the church rules (that had nothing to do with the Word of God), being preached about from the pulpit, or sat down and not allowed to serve in any capacity.

In an environment where blind obedience is expected and independent thought and individuality was discouraged, it became a challenge and awfully difficult to grow and mature under that type of leadership. Recently, while welcoming new members, I was shocked and saddened to hear that there are still ministries where the people are so bound that the pastor is not only telling women that they cannot wear pants, makeup, and earrings, but they also can't wear weaves or braid their hair! The idea that a pastor would tell a woman what hairstyle to wear is unbelievable. That stuff doesn't bring anyone closer to Jesus; it doesn't help members grow or mature. These kinds of manipulative tactics, controlling where members go, what they wear, how they live their private lives, raise their children, and what goes on in a married couples' bedroom are some of the attributes of an insecure leader and signs that you're in an unhealthy environment.

Do you look forward to going to church or does your anxiety level rise, bringing on a feeling of dread? When you're in service, do you feel free to worship, or do you feel bound and unable to express yourself? Does the pastor preach an uplifting message, from the Word of God, that even if it challenges or corrects you, it still gives you hope and is presented with sincere love and compassion? Or did the pastor fuss and beat up on everyone with a message of condemnation? And, finally, are you ashamed or afraid to invite someone to your church, or when you did, were you embarrassed or had to apologize to your guests because of something that was said or done at your church? It's very difficult to grow and mature properly in an unhealthy environment like that.

In Luke's gospel, the young child Jesus is described as continuing to grow and becoming strong in spirit, filled with wisdom, and having the grace (favor, spiritual blessing of God)

upon Him. So not only did Jesus, like all of us, have to grow and mature physically, but He had to grow spiritually as well. In fact, when we see Him in Luke 2:41-52, at the age of twelve, after having been left behind in Jerusalem by His parents, Jesus had matured to the point where teachers were astonished by His intelligence, understanding, and answers. At the end of the chapter, verse fifty-two says, "and Jesus kept increasing in wisdom and in favor with God and man."

As people of God, we have the same ability to continually grow and mature spiritually, to increase in wisdom and experience. Life has a way of constantly teaching us lessons and providing tests, trials, and challenges that must be passed, endured, and overcome. All of us can look at various moments in our lives that were extremely difficult; it may have been a rough childhood, an unstable household, abusive relationships, financial hardships, loss of a loved one, illness, or physical disability. As devastating as they were (and in some cases are currently) they proved to be a reservoir from which we've drawn strength, courage, wisdom, and experience. They helped us to as 2 Peter 3:18 says, "grow in grace and knowledge of our Lord Jesus Christ," and they revealed some things to us about ourselves and some things about the Lord. They showed us that we had more strength than we thought and how powerful Christ is in our lives. Those things we learned from our past experiences can be viewed in the same way we looked at tests, pop quizzes, and final exams when we were in school; they let us know what we knew and what we didn't know. Sometimes they were the deciding factor in whether you graduated or not.

After being baptized by John the Baptist, but before Jesus began his ministry, the gospel describes how the Holy Spirit led him into the wilderness to be tempted by Satan. After a powerful spiritual experience, the Spirit brought Jesus to a place of testing. After fasting for forty days and forty nights, He overcame the enemy by speaking the Word of God that had been instilled in Him from childhood. In the same way, we also can learn and grow through our trials and tribulations and use them to propel us into our destiny and purpose. In the book of James, he writes, "Consider it pure joy, my brothers and sisters, whenever you face trials of many kinds, because you know that the testing of your faith produces perseverance. Let perseverance finish its work so that you may be mature and complete, not lacking anything." He's encouraging believers to view their difficulties in a different light, that we should realize that trials are producing a greater level of maturity and helping us become complete, fully developed men and women of God.

The things you were exposed to as well as what you were prevented from experiencing can have a lasting effect on us as we grow older. Recently, while teaching Bible study, we began discussing what it was like being raised in a strict, old school church environment. After we talked about how women couldn't wear pants, jewelry, or makeup, it dawned on me how the church rules affected me personally. I realized that I never learned how to play cards, because they weren't allowed in our house. We also couldn't play games that used dice, so Monopoly® was off limits.

But the way I may have been most impacted was when it comes to my love for music. Secular music wasn't allowed in our home, with the exception of my father, who listened to classical and easy-listening music, and my brothers Darryl and Michael, who had a stereo component record player in their bedroom. We were also blessed to have a portable radio that was given to us by our maternal grandmother, which we kept in what became the boys bathroom and where I heard the debut single, "I Want You Back" by this new group, The Jackson 5. For a great portion of my childhood, we could only listen to music at home when my parents were gone. Of course, that meant making a mad dash to turn down the music once we heard their car pulling up. This was during the late sixties and throughout the mid seventies when arguably some of the best music ever was released. I envied my friends that had the freedom to listen to music and had these classic albums in their homes.

However, there were a few things that helped me survive and cultivate the passion for music that I have today. First, my dad gave me several transistor radios, through the years, so I could listen to sports, especially the Dodgers and Lakers. I would keep the radio under my pillow and listen to AM Pop Radio stations that helped broadened my musical knowledge beyond R&B. Secondly, I was able to listen to my brother's records in their room, on low or with headphones, while reading all the liner notes, feeding my musical knowledge. Finally, it changed with my mother, when in 1977 while I was in Jr. High, a classmate of mine named Angie, typed up the lyrics to one of my all-time favorite songs, "As" by Stevie Wonder, from the "Songs in the Key of Life" album. I left the lyrics on the dresser in my bedroom and my mother saw them and asked me about them. She thought it was a poem, and to my surprise, she liked them! I told her it was a Stevie Wonder song and she reiterated how much she liked it. That let me know that music wasn't a sin and that it was OK to listen to it.

That night in Bible study, I realized that because they had kept me from listening to music and going to movies, it made me want to find out what I had missed out on. I became a student of various musical genres, and I have a vast music library with thousands of songs and most of the classic albums I couldn't listen to as a child. Another blessing that came out of this situation was my ability to memorize lyrics and liner notes became extremely refined, to the point where I could play entire albums in my head. I believe that happened because it had been kept from me for so long. When we became parents, Carla and I raised our children, Angela and Randall, in a very different way. The things that they experienced and were exposed to helped them become more balanced and well-rounded adults.

Being raised in a spiritual environment with God-fearing parents and lots of love and support is the primary reason why I am the man I am today, but the things I wasn't allowed to experience or participate in also had a significant impact on my life. Our upbringing, society, and the church, in addition to our exposure and experiences, can all play a vital role in our growth and development.

Chapter 2

Mature Environments:
When I Was a Child

*E*very now and then, it is good for us to look within our-selves and make an honest assessment of where we are and where we have been. We need to be brutally honest when dealing with what is in our hearts and minds. We should look at our growth and development, go back as far as we can, and chart our progress from the time we were children. Hopefully, when you look back you can see that great strides have been made since the time you were a child.

In the next several chapters, I'll examine and break down 1 Corinthians 13:11 and its examples of natural growth and relating that to our spiritual growth. In 1 Corinthians 13, the apostle Paul is talking to the church about the greatest gift: charity or agape love. He talks about the fact that love never fails; other gifts may cease but love lasts forever. In verse 11 he says, "When I was a child, I spake as a child, I understood as a child, I thought as child, but when I became a man, I put away childish things." Here we have Paul looking back over his life and acknowledging that he had to go through various stages of development to reach maturity. How he spoke, understood, and thought evolved over time, as he matured and as his relationship with Christ became stronger. He matured to the point where he could put off childish and immature practices and be-haviors. You and I are not exempt from the development process; how we speak, understand, and think should change as we go through the natural stages of development (newborn, infant, toddler, child, adolescent, teen, adult). We also go through spiritual and emotional development, where we will have to evaluate our behaviors and no longer practice them, and "put them away."

You may never know by looking at us on any given Sunday morning at church, but we haven't always been as mature as we appear today. We may have had several major challenges to overcome naturally as well as spiritually. Maybe you were raised in a single-parent household with limited resources, but the family found a way, through perseverance and hard work, to not only survive but thrive. Or maybe you had both parents, but it still wasn't a loving household and you had to depend on people that God placed in your life to show you the love and care that everyone needs. It could have been a situation where you weren't healthy physically or had psychological challenges, but your family connected with the right people at the right time, that helped you meet the challenges head on and conquer them. We can all look back at our childhood experiences in the natural and be grateful that we made it through.

In the same way, we can look back to a time when we were spiritually immature. We may not have received the proper care when we were born again. Everyone in the church might not have been loving or nurturing, but the Lord placed that one person in your life that became the one friend you needed to stay encouraged. Maybe God gave you a great love for His Word, or you loved to worship, and even though it was a struggle to get to church, worship and the Word of God kept you coming back and helped you hang in there, while you were growing spiritually. Finally, you may have been hurt by someone in church when you were a babe in Christ, and your first instinct was to lash out and then leave because you were wounded. But the Lord provided a pathway to healing by sending a person into your life to bring healing and comfort and to get you to focus on Jesus instead of the one that hurt you.

As you look back to the time when you were a child naturally and spiritually, you can truly say, you've come a long way and you don't look like what you've been through. You can also see how much you've grown, and you might even smile when you recall how you reacted and behaved back in the day. You'll also be grateful and thankful to God for keeping you while you were growing and developing into the mature person you are today.

As spiritual leaders, it is critical for us to make sure our ministries provide an atmosphere that challenges, encourages, trains, and empowers its members to be great in God. Leaders can ensure that their members are in an environment where they can grow and mature, by first, continuing to learn and grow themselves. Pastors and leaders should continue to read, take classes, attend conferences and symposiums that challenge, empower, instruct, and stretch them individually. Once the leader has been exposed to better, then they can bring their members to another level.

When I was a young minister, soon to be pastor, my life and ministry were transformed by two major events: 1) attending Aenon Bible College (Aenon) at Home Assembly Church in Los Angeles in 1988 and 2) going to Bishop Norman L. Wagner's "Pentecost in Perspective" (PIP) Conference in Youngstown, Ohio in 1992. Coming from a small church, I was exposed to ministry at Aenon on a level I had never experienced before. I got a chance to see how large churches operated in addition to being able to glean wisdom and knowledge from great leaders. I also developed a deep love for the Word of God and learned the importance of studying and sermon preparation. I also connected with people that have had a lifelong impact on me.

At PIP, I learned how to pastor and lead people on a whole new level. Bishop Norman L. Wagner taught us and more importantly, showed us how to organize our staff, as well as the importance of being in the right place, at the right time, with the right attitude. I learned how to lead people into the presence of God and to hear the voice of God and flow in the Spirit. I was then able to take the things I had learned and been exposed to and bring them back home and pour them into the leaders and members of my church. Also, these two events taught me how to create an atmosphere where growth was not only welcomed but was encouraged.

Does that mean that everyone got it and were mature Christians? Not! In fact, I was not completely mature as a leader myself and still made mistakes, but the environment and culture had changed to the point where our church was growing in numbers, and more importantly, growing spiritually. Their growth became evident in how many of them handled adversity; they exercised faith, prayed and used the Word of God, on their own, without depending on the assistance of the church elders. Their level of support of the ministry's vision and willingness to serve were also signs of spiritual growth. Once I understood the importance of my personal growth and maturity and that of my staff and leaders is when it became easier to manage and facilitate the growth of the ministry. The most rewarding experience I have as a pastor is to see the growth and development of members, and to see them become spiritually mature Christians.

My wife, Carla and I have been married for thirty-three years, and she has been an educator in the Los Angeles Unified School District almost as long. She has almost exclusively taught kindergarteners or first graders (5 or 6 years old) her entire career. She introduced me to a method that teachers use to instruct young children called "Developmentally Appropriate," where they assign tasks that fit a child's age group. You would not have a preschooler try to copy assignments from the blackboard; you would have them work in a writing circle with colored paper, markers, and pencils. As they grow, develop, and mature, the way you teach them begins to change as well; you instruct them according to their abilities, age, and how they fit in certain developmental norms. Just as educators know their students' capabilities and instruct them in a developmentally appropriate way, it is important for pastors and leaders to know what is developmentally appropriate for God's people. If a student is given a task that is above their level, they will become frustrated and discouraged and may even act out. Pastors must be mindful to lead, teach, instruct, and create an environment for God's people, and shepherd them in a way that does not overwhelm them, but nurtures and sparks them to grow and become what God has called them to be.

One of the challenges of pastoring is finding a way to help members grow who are at different levels of maturity. How do you avoid overwhelming the less mature, while at the same time inspiring the spiritually mature to an even greater level? The amazing thing I learned about the Gospel of Christ, is that when it's presented with love, passion, clarity, and intelligence, coupled with an understanding of the human condition, the message will reach people right where they are. My assignment when I preach, teach, or present is to make sure that I've heard from God and that I have respect for the members, and deliver the message in a way that children, seniors, and everyone in between can receive and relate to it. When the message is relatable, the mature and immature can grow, at the same time.

When I enrolled at Aenon Bible College in January 1988, I had no idea that my life was about to change forever. My friend, Brian Singleton, a fellow associate minister at El Bethel had enrolled the previous semester and he encouraged me to join him. It would prove to be a bonding experience since we would carpool every Monday night after we got home from work. It would also spark me to become a true student of the scriptures and enable me to become a much more effective preacher, teacher, and leader. At that time, I had a lot on my plate—I was working at the Post Office delivering mail, I was a young minister and Youth President at church, as well as I was becoming active in the Youth Department of the California/Nevada/Hawaii District Council of our parent organization, the Pentecostal Assemblies of the World (PAW). In addition to all those things, Carla and I were still basically newlyweds, since we'd only been married two and a half years and were still learning what marriage was all about.

Spending time with Brian on the drives to and from school helped us become more like brothers rather than friends. It would become an important part of my development as a young married man of God. We would have great conversations where we would encourage one another, sharing laughs as well as some great food (Brian knew some great late-night spots.) We were around each other so much people were shocked when they saw one of us without the other. Hanging out with Brian also helped ease my transition into the culture at Aenon. Since I was a very quiet and somewhat reserved individual from a small church in the San Fernando Valley suburbs of Los Angeles, I didn't say very much at all. Brian, on the other hand, was very outgoing and seemed to know everyone; he introduced me to so many people, I soon found myself with a whole new set of friends.

My first class, Old Testament Survey, with the incomparable Dean of Aenon, Norma L. Jackson, was so addictive, I would tell people it was like the old commercial slogan for Lay's Potato Chips, "Nobody Can Eat Just One." Once you took her class, you'd be hooked. I was quite content sitting way in the back of the class with my mouth shut. I was new and many of the other students seemed to be more advanced and had been attending much longer than me. Dean Jackson's class was amazing; I was learning so much and beginning to grow and develop as a minister and leader. I was inspired to study the Word on a new level, and I could see the results in the effectiveness of my teaching and preaching.

Everything was going well, when one day early in the Fall semester, Dean Jackson announced that they would be holding elections for Student Body Officers and they were taking nominations. I relaxed as I sat back in my chair, thinking to myself, there's no way I'm going to put my name in for nomination, this is only my second semester here. At that moment, Dean Jackson spoke the words that would change my life. She cried from the front of the classroom, "Bro. Hamilton, come on up here and put your name in for one of these offices." I was shocked, but I knew I had to be obedient and I also had to think fast. I submitted my name for the position of Vice President (Social Affairs), thinking there was no way I was going to win, but much to my surprise, I did! This gave me my first leadership opportunity outside of my local church. It also allowed me to be connected with some of the most intelligent, gifted, capable, and kind people I've ever known. Two of them: Bernadette Green (Baity) and David Anderson, both became lifelong friends, and pushed, encouraged, and helped me develop and mature into a more effective leader. The experiences I had at Aenon helped prepare me for the positions I'm in today and helped me become a better leader, pastor, and friend.

Even if we aren't born into an environment that's conducive for our growth and maturity, the Lord can reposition us to a place where we develop and become spiritually mature.

Chapter 3

Mature Speech:
I Spake as a Child

*I*t is amazing that in this age of social networking, smart phones, interactive computers, and televisions, that we have trouble communicating effectively. It seems as if we do not know how to speak to one another anymore, especially face to face.

It is imperative that members of the Body of Christ understand that what we say is what we get! When our speech lacks clarity and authority or is negative and foolish, we fail to become the person we should be and possess what we should have.

Too often we get caught up in silly childish discussions over irrelevant issues which do not help us grow. In 2 Timothy 2:14b, 16, and 23 (NIV), Paul warns the young bishop Timothy to,

> "warn them before God against quarreling about words; it is of no value, and only ruins those who listen. Avoid godless chatter, because those who indulge in it will become more and more ungodly. Don't have anything to do with foolish and stupid arguments, because you know they produce quarrels."

We can clearly see from these scriptures that Paul understood the problems that arise from immature speech. We cannot allow ourselves to get caught up in talk that does not edify.

Proverbs 18:21 teaches that, "Death and life are in the power of the tongue." Many times, we have spoken life to things which should die and death to things that should live. How often have we let negative words kill a blessing God had ordained for us? How many times have we talked ourselves out of healing, deliverance, education, and breakthrough? How often do we give life to someone else's negativity by repeating their doubts, fears, or unbelief? Never allow yourself to be anyone's dumping ground. Do not let other people's fears and lack of faith influence you.

When we speak words of faith, we operate with the authority and confidence Jesus said we should have. In Mark 11:20-26, we find the account of Jesus speaking to an unfruitful fig tree. He spoke audibly to the tree, cursing it forever. When Jesus and the apostles returned the next day and saw the tree dried up from the roots, He told them to have faith in God, speak to the mountain, doubting nothing, and you will have whatsoever you say. Your words are powerful; when you speak like the mature child of God you are, get ready for your life to change. Speak that thing and it shall come to pass!

We hear quite often that our words have power, but Proverbs 18:20-21 lets us know words also have consequences. Verse 20 says, "A man's stomach will be satisfied with the fruit of his mouth; he will be satisfied with the consequences of his words." (Proverbs 18:20AMP) What we speak determines what we produce and harvest. Our words matter! For example, I have had to be careful and mindful of what I say even when I am preaching and teaching. I have caught myself saying things like, "Y'all aren't hearing me" or "You're not getting this." I under-stand that some of that is just the way preachers talk in church, but it dawned on me, that if I keep saying those types of things, they will become reality. Now I make a conscious effort to work on not saying, "The Lord is about to" or "is going to do some-thing"; instead, I say, "The Lord is doing this or that."

In Matthew 8:5-13, we read the account of the Roman centurion who came to Jesus asking Him to heal his suffering servant, who was at the centurion's home. Jesus says, "I will come and heal him"; the centurion's replies, "I'm not worthy that you shouldest come under my roof, but speak the word only and my servant shall be healed." (Matthew 8:8 KJV) He realized that the words of Jesus, the Son of God, have authority and that whatever Jesus said would come to pass. Jesus said, "I have not found so great faith, no not in all Israel." The lesson for you and me as mature children of God is that what we believe and the things we say have power and consequences. Our lives will become the reality of what we speak into existence.

Chapter 4

Mature Thinking:
I Understood as a Child

*A*s we continue to break down 1 Corinthians 13:11, it is important to pause here and define the word translated as *"understood"* in the KJV. The Greek word for understood is *"phronéō"* which actually means *"to think."*

If we are to develop into mature Christians, it must start in our minds. Our thinking must change. As Romans 12:2 states, "be ye transformed by the renewing of your mind." How we think impacts every aspect of our lives, naturally and spiritually. The mind is also the battleground where the enemy wages war, sets up strongholds, imaginations, and "every high thing that exalteth itself against the knowledge of God." (2 Corinthians 10:4-5)

Have you ever noticed how difficult it is for an immature thinker to stay focused or sit still? One day they are focused on taking ballet, the next day piano lessons. Oftentimes they are influenced by the latest fad or what they have seen their friends doing. The same problems parents face when dealing with a precocious child or teen can be found in the body of Christ among adults. I've seen adults throwing tantrums, having pity parties, pouting, engaging in public shouting matches and nearly coming to blows at church! I've seen individuals leave the church because they couldn't get their way or because they had been removed from a position. I can't count how many times I've dealt with two grownups that were upset because one didn't speak to the other. I've seen pastors, leaders, and even bishops engaging in childish, immature behavior. I'm also speaking from personal experience. I haven't always behaved in a spiritually mature manner; I've been impatient and impulsive; I have gotten distracted and wasted time, energy, and money. Thank God for not giving up on me and for bringing me back in line. My experiences taught me how to be patient and to help those that are struggling to grow up spiritually.

When we overcome immature thinking, we move away from being self-centered, self-absorbed carnal Christians and begin to operate in God's divine will. We are no longer wrapped up in what we want but are submissive to and led by God.

We must also be careful about the things we allow our minds to entertain. Foolish, silly thoughts and issues cannot have a place in the mature Christian mind. Time must not be wasted on insignificant, petty things. Doubts, fears, and anxieties must be given completely to the Lord. Philippians 4:6-7 (NIV) admonishes us to,

> "Do not be anxious about anything, but in every situation, by prayer and petition, with thanksgiving, present your requests to God. And the peace of God, which transcends all understanding, will guard your hearts and your minds in Christ Jesus."

Do not worry about anything but pray about everything! Do not allow negative thoughts to dominate your thinking. Do not let other folks' negativity or unbelief rest in your mind and spirit. Our minds should stay focused on "whatever is true, whatever is noble, whatever is right, whatever is pure, whatever is lovely, whatever is admirable—if anything is excellent or praiseworthy—think about such things." (Philippians 4:8, NIV)

In the winter of 1979, when I was a 10th grader, I used to ride one of the several buses that took predominately African American students from the Pacoima/San Fernando area to a school in Granada Hills. As a somewhat quiet (isolated, since most of my friends went to another school) fourteen-year-old, what made the otherwise anxious ride bearable was the fact that we had cool bus drivers that liked music (as much as I do) and filled the buses with the R&B sounds played on the local radio station, 1580 KDAY.

One day the DJ played a new single from a band named "Switch," who was about to release their second album, after their very successful debut. The new single was titled, "I Call Your Name." The lead singer and songwriter was Bobby De-Barge, who started the song intro,

> "I used to think about immature things. You know like, do you love me? Do you want me? Are you gonna call me like you said you would? Is this really your real phone number? But you know I'm a man now baby, a grown man, and I came a long way he-he. And experience taught me one thing, taught me to hold on to my love." (Bobby DeBarge)

The thing about these lyrics that got my attention as a somewhat girl-crazy teenage boy was those were the same silly questions I was asking and thinking. But I realized that my thinking was immature. I also realized that I can no longer afford to keep thinking like an adolescent My thinking had to change and my mind had to mature. Not only was I growing physically, I also needed to develop mature social skills.

When we are immature in our thinking, we waste time on small, petty, and insignificant issues. I have seen grown people in church behave like silly teenagers; they pout if they are not receiving the attention or acknowledgement they think they deserve; they get upset if someone did not speak to them first or left them out of an activity. They allow themselves to drown in the pool of self-pity and dwell on trivial issues for far too long, fostering negative thoughts to build up to the point where they cannot function.

As our thinking matures, we should become more aware of our thoughts and learn how to put things into perspective and focus on the things and people that really matter.

Chapter 5

Mature Reasoning:
I Thought as a Child

The word *"logizomal"* is translated as *"thought"* in the KJV and means *to reason*. It is derived from logos, meaning intelligence, a word as the expression of intelligent thought. This is important because it deals with how we link and put together inward thoughts and feelings. Are we able to think logically and rationally?

Immaturity has an impact on how we put our thoughts together. When we are immature, we are not as logical in our thinking. We tend to think and react based on emotion instead of logic. Children often react in an emotional fashion when things do not go their way. They do not process information in a logical, rational fashion. They will also throw tantrums or pout if they do not get their way. When adults react emotionally, we say they are being childish or immature; often they will do something dramatic to get attention, just like children.

Early experiences can have a lasting impact on how we process information and react to situations. Many times, our formative environment has an influence on one's thinking.

We must avoid falling into cycles or ruts where we draw the same conclusions and react emotionally or irrationally. Believe it or not, we can reach a level of spiritual growth and maturity that we begin to view trials, tribulations, and challenges differently. In James 1:2-4 (AMP), he writes,

> "Consider it nothing but joy, my brothers and sisters whenever you fall into various trials. Be assured that the testing of your faith [through experience] produces endurance [leading to spiritual maturity, and inner peace]. And let endurance have its perfect result and do a thorough work, so that you may be perfect and completely developed [in your faith], lacking in nothing."

When our thinking changes, we won't find ourselves repeating patterns of self-doubt or becoming angry or depressed because we're facing another challenge or roadblock. We won't be quick to jump to conclusions or believe the worst about every situation. No, when our thinking changes, we can "consider it joy" when things go wrong, because we know that the same God that brought us out the last time will definitely do it again. We'll look at the trial as the latest test and we'll pass this one, too. The trials that we've already overcome provide us with wisdom and experience as well as the knowledge that every challenge we face teaches us valuable lessons about God and about ourselves.

When we reach that level of maturity, we break the cycle of illogical reasoning and generational influences. We come out of the rut of emotional, immature reactions and free ourselves from the shackles of drama.

Have you ever been guilty of overthinking and dwelling on an issue or overreacted to something someone said to you or about you, only to learn that the thing you were worried about was not true or never actually happened? I have lost sleep, worried myself sick, lost my cool, and panicked over things that were like The Temptations classic, "Just My Imagination (Running Away With Me.)"

In the song, the lead singer, Eddie Kendricks, sings about this woman that he is in love with. He sings,

"Each day through my window I watch her as she passes by
I say to myself you're such a lucky guy,
To have a girl like her is truly a dream come true
Out of all the fellows in the world she belongs to me."

Then the chorus says:

> "But it was Just my imagination,
> once again runnin' away with me."

The beautiful picture pained by the lyrics in the verses stand in stark contrast to the reality of the chorus. In fact, by the end of the song, he admits, "But in reality, she doesn't even know me."

One of the most endearing characteristics of children is their vivid, sometimes, wild imaginations. They have big dreams and believe that anything is possible. Their wild imaginations can oftentimes venture into some scary places where they imagine monsters or things they see on TV or in movies will come and do them harm. But as they grow older and mature, and with the help of reassuring adults, they realize their fears were unfounded and that they had nothing to worry about.

It can also work the same way for believers as we grow and develop spiritually. We can find ourselves upset and worried about things that aren't real. In 2 Corinthians 10:5, Paul writes that our spiritual weapons are able to, "Cast down imaginations and every high thing that exalts itself against the knowledge of God." The battleground is our mind; this is where spiritual warfare takes place, and where the enemy tries to launch an attack with strongholds which are like spiritual "Walls of Jericho," fortresses preventing negative thoughts from getting out and positive thoughts from getting in; and imaginations, as well as high things or barriers which prevent the knowledge of God from getting through. When we are immature, doubt, fear, and anxiety can override our faith, causing us to react to things that are not real. We start playing out scenarios and preparing for consequences that never actually happen.

But just like when you were a kid and the adults in your life helped you grow up and mature and you realized that there was not anything to be afraid of, when you grow in God and believe His Word, you can begin to pull down mental strongholds that have prevented you from becoming the person you were destined to be. You can cast down imaginations—those things that paralyzed you with fear and anxiety and prevented you from moving forward and walking in your purpose. Finally, you can cast down every high thing that blocks the knowledge of God, keeping you from knowing who you are in Him, and who He wants to be in your life.

Chapter 6

Mature Response:
Put Away Childish Things

*T*here comes a time in each of our lives when we realize we are not kids anymore. Maybe it was when you moved out of your parents' house or when you got married. It could have been when the bills started coming in the mail with your name on them or even when your first child was born. There are moments in your life where you realize I am grown and not a kid anymore. We must come to grips with a couple of facts.

1) We are adults.

2) We must put our toys away.

Growth is not measured by age or how long you have been in a particular place. Nor can it be measured by people around you. Growth can be charted by how you respond to challenges and accept responsibility. This applies naturally and spiritually.

A good indicator of one's growth is the ability to identify and deal with (put away) childish things. Can I look at them for what they are? Can I put them in their proper place? Do I have the right perspective as it relates to its importance?

There are clear indicators that you have grown up. One of the first changes you notice is how you respond to different challenges that come your way. When an immature individual faces adversity or does not get their way, they can pout or throw a tantrum and act out, to let everyone know they are upset. In the past, when a relationship came to an end, you were not able to function for a month while you had a pity party. Also, when we are spiritually immature, we emphasize the importance of inconsequential things. We like to spend time engaging in activities that may feel good for the moment but do not get us any closer to God or advance His Kingdom. But when you have matured, you do not panic or go off on others. You handle the ups and downs and highs and lows of life with grace, knowing that trouble does not last always, and the same God that brought you through before will do it again. Little things that seemed so important before are placed into proper perspective, and you are more mindful of where you expend your energy and to whom you give your time, money, and attention.

Strange as it may seem, keys can be one way to chart our growth and maturity. When I was a kid and still in elementary school, my mother and father were both working during the day and my older brothers were attending Jr. High, so that meant I had to be responsible for my little sister, Valerie, and make sure we both got home safely from school. We were a group of children which would later be referred to as "latchkey kids," children that had to come home from school and take care of themselves until one of their parents or an older sibling came home. We had to lock the door behind us, change out of our school clothes, get a snack, and start our homework. We were not allowed to leave the house and we could not have any visitors. It was at that moment that I received my first key and the responsibility to look after my sister. My parents believed that I was mature enough to keep my sister and later on my younger brother, Randy, safe. I realized early on that when you are given keys, a level of responsibility comes with it.

In Matthew 16:13-19, we find Jesus questioning His disciples, while in the coasts of Caesarea and Philippi (a powerful region of Greco-Roman oppression). He asked them, "Whom do men say that I the Son of Man am?" They responded, "Some say thou are John the Baptist, some say Elijah and others Jeremiah or one of the prophets." Jesus proceeded to ask the important question, "Whom do you say I am?" Peter boldly declared, "Thou art the Christ, the Son of The Living God!"

Jesus commends Peter and declares to all the apostles that upon that truth (that He was the Christ), He was building a church that "the gates of hell couldn't prevail against it." Then Jesus declares He is transferring the keys to the kingdom of heaven: and whatsoever you bind on earth, shall be bound in heaven and whatsoever you loose on earth, will be loosed in heaven." He was giving them and the church that would follow them spiritual authority and the responsibility to accomplish His will and advance His kingdom on earth. Mature believers still have the keys, or spiritual authority, and the people of God still have power to bind and loose situations, spirits, and circumstances according to God's divine Will. The Lord continues to use mature men and women to advance His kingdom through prayer, sharing our faith, helping the poor, and demonstrating God's love to the world.

These days, the way we gain and limit access to many of our most valuable possessions has changed dramatically. For example, my wife and I can both unlock and operate our cars by simply having our keys in our possession, and we start the engine by pushing a button. That's a long way from my first car, a 1973 Chevy Impala, that had a separate key for the ignition and the trunk. We can now use facial recognition, codes, fingerprints, and even our voices to access buildings, unlock our phones, turn on appliances, unlock and start our vehicles, and lock our houses.

The same holds true when it comes to using the keys of the kingdom and exercising our spiritual authority. If we possess the Spirit of God and have faith in Him and His Word as well as the authority of the name of Jesus, we will have binding and loosing power and gain access to what He has for us. The keys, authority, and access to many of the blessings the Lord has for us are also voice activated. When we use mature speech as we pray, speak God's Word, and decree and declare positive things over our lives the way Jesus did, we gain access to the mind of God, and He empowers us to do His will "on earth, as it is in heaven."

When some of us were first saved, we may have spent a great deal of our time wondering whether we could participate in certain activities and still be saved; wondering how close we could get to sin without going too far. Is this a sin? But when you mature, you are more concerned with getting closer to God than you are about what you can get away with.

Your level of responsibility and accountability changes as you mature. Instead of placing blame on someone else or passing the buck, you learn to accept greater responsibility. Being accountable for your decisions and actions should also develop as one matures.

As mature believers, we must not only grow in grace and favor with God but also with our fellow man. If we examine the life of Jesus, we can see that He not only grew physically ("And the child grew and became strong; he was filled with wisdom, and the grace of God was on him" Luke 2:40, NIV), but He had favor with God and man ("And Jesus grew in wisdom and stature, and in favor with God and man." Luke 2:52, NIV). We should be mature in our dealings with fellow believers and also non-believers.

When we are growing in favor with God and man, when we begin to grow spiritually and understand that God's Hand is resting on us, we will not be the only one who notices. When we become aware of our increased spiritual maturity and that the favor and grace of God is on us, our attitude and outlook will change. This grace and favor are present because we have spent more time in God's presence, increased our study of His

Word, and have applied the things that we have learned in our everyday lives. Others will notice your change in attitude and positive outlook, and it will begin to manifest itself in all aspects of our lives. You will have an effect on everyone you come in contact with.

Putting childish things away does not mean that you become stiff, boring, or super serious. We should always have a part of us that is youthful and whimsical. We have to know how to have fun and be playful; that will be good for us as we get older, but it should not be the dominant part of our character.

We must resist the temptations to indulge in childish, immature behavior and habits. Paul warned Timothy to, "Flee the evil desires of youth, and pursue righteousness, faith, love, and peace . . ." (2 Timothy 2:22, NIV). We must pray for strength and courage to put away the childish things in our lives and pursue the love of God. Love becomes the most important characteristic of a mature Christian. In 1 Corinthians 13, Paul talked about faith, hope, and love, and concluded that the greatest is love. When we are showing the kind of love described in 1 Corinthians 13, we have matured into a child of God. When John spoke of 'perfect love' casting out fear (1 John 4:18), he was speaking of a 'mature' or 'fully developed' love—God's love being demonstrated in our lives to the point where "as he is, so are we in this world" (1 John 4:17). When we reach this place of maturity, we will have no fear of judgment and we will be made 'perfect' in love.

Chapter 7

Mature Leaders:
Solid Food for the Mature

*P*aul, the writer of Hebrews, admonishes the Hebrew believer for no longer trying to understand and being dull and sluggish in their spiritual hearing, and in need of milk instead of meat or solid food. He stated that "solid food is for the mature, who by constant use have trained themselves to distinguish good from evil." (Hebrews 5:14, NIV) He felt like they should have been more fully developed and should be able to teach others.

Believers must realize there is more to our walk with Christ than being "churchy,"—in other words placing more importance on emotional expressions of dancing and shouting in our services or rallying around basic doctrinal issues like water baptism and the infilling of the Holy Spirit. These things are all important parts of the worship experience and the salvation process, but there is more to our relationship with Christ than these basic principles. Leaders must take us beyond the elementary teachings and lead us to perfection or maturity. Hebrews 6:1-3 (AMP) says,

> "Therefore let us get past the elementary stage in the teachings about Christ, advancing on to maturity and perfection and spiritual completeness [doing this], without laying again a foundation of repentance from dead works and of faith toward God, of teaching about washings (ritual purifications), the laying on of hands, the resurrection of the dead and eternal judgment. [These are all important matters in which you should have been proficient long ago.] And we will do this [that is proceed to maturity], if God permits."

Sometimes our ministries spend too much time going over basic principles of the doctrine (repentance, baptism, etc.) and never move God's people beyond that to maturity.

When Jesus was starting His earthly ministry, after He had gathered a large number of converts, He selected twelve apostles that he empowered and trained to carry the kingdom message to the world. He took this group of ordinary men, with different backgrounds, occupations, and experiences and formed the pillars of the church. He gave today's pastors and leaders an example of how to develop a team of leaders that would not only be effective in the time that they lived but would have an impact forever.

In Luke 5:1-11, we see Jesus calling four of His disciples–Simon Peter, Andrew, James, and John–into ministry. They were already disciples, but they were still on their jobs as fishermen. As the crowd pressed upon Jesus, He sat in Peter's boat and taught the multitude, while the disciples washed their fishing nets after an unsuccessful night of fishing. When He was finished teaching, Jesus tells Peter to "launch out into the deep" and let down his nets for a large catch of fish. Peter tells Him they had toiled all night and hadn't caught anything, but "at his word" he'd launch out. They caught an overwhelming number of fish, so many that their net began to break, their boat began to sink, and they had to call their partners to help them get the catch to shore. Jesus tells them from now on, you'll be "fishers of men." They were so impacted by Jesus that they left everything and followed Him. Leaders have to be able to effectively empower men and women to reach this level of maturity to advance the Kingdom of God.

As leaders and as part of the five-fold ministry (apostles, prophets, evangelists, pastors, and teachers), we must understand that the Lord has positioned us to fully equip and perfect His people for works of service and to build up the body of

Christ. We must be diligent about leading and feeding, pouring into people, and helping them grow in faith and in love. Ephesians 4:13-16, AMP, says it like this,

> "Until we all reach oneness in the faith and in the knowledge of the Son of God [growing spiritually] to become a mature believer, reaching the measure of the fullness of Christ [manifesting His spiritual completeness and exercising our spiritual gifts in unity]. So that we are no longer children [spiritually immature], tossed back and forth [like ships on a stormy sea] and carried about by every wind of [shifting] doctrine by the cunning and trickery of [unscrupulous] men, by the deceitful scheming of people ready to do anything [for personal profit]. But speaking the truth in love [in all things – both our speech and our lives expressing His truth], let us grow up in all things into Him [following His example] who is the Head – Christ. From Him the whole body (the church, in all its various parts), joined and knitted firmly together by what every joint supplies, when each part is working properly, causes the body to grow and mature, building itself up in [unselfish] love."

We have to always be mindful of the fact that we are here to help, strengthen, and minister to the people that are connected to us.

The Greek word for perfection in Hebrews 6 is "teleios," which means adult, full grown, and mature. We must be mature in every aspect of our lives. Not only should we be able to discern between good and evil but also in how we treat one another; growing in grace and knowledge of Christ and also sharing His love and power with the world.

As we begin to mature, the Word of God will give us revelations, visions, and a greater understanding of His will for our lives. We should also be ready to operate with greater authority and responsibility. Kingdom speaking, thinking, and reasoning will transform individuals, families, churches, and communities.

Every believer has a responsibility to

"add to your faith goodness; and to your goodness knowledge; and to knowledge, self-control; and to self-control, perseverance; and to perseverance godliness; and to godliness, brotherly kindness; and to brother kindness, love. For if you possess these qualities in increasing measure, they will keep you from being ineffective and unproductive in your knowledge of our Lord Jesus Christ . . . for if you do these things, you will never fall." (2 Peter 1:5-8, 10, NIV)

The principles outlined in the first chapter of Second Peter tell us we've been given everything we need for a dynamic spiritual life and the ability to flourish in our everyday lives. We must tap into that power by constantly adding to our faith in very practical ways, such as being kind and patient, developing self-control and showing love to one another.

My prayer is that each of us realizes that no one can do this for you; each of us must become an active participant in our own developmental process. Let's go on to perfection and receive everything that the Lord has ordained for us.

Believers are not exempt from responsibility. They must understand that they have been given gifts and gifted people (apostles, prophets, evangelists, pastors, and teachers) to help them grow, develop, and become all that God has destined them to be, and to live an abundant life while walking in their divine purpose. Not only has God given us leaders as ministry gifts, but He has fully equipped us with absolutely everything necessary to be effective in Kingdom building.

Chapter 8

Mature Relationships:
Love Takes Serious Work

erious relationships and marriage are for grown folks. Over the course of my career as a pastor, leader, and marriage counselor, I've found myself having to repeat that phrase on numerous occasions. Nowadays, it seems like it's getting more and more difficult to make relationships work, not just in society, but it's also becoming more common in the church, with the laity and pastors alike. We're finding an ever-increasing number of couples calling it quits.

I believe maturity, or the lack thereof, plays a major role in the increased divorce rates and separations we're seeing in society. When individuals enter into marriage or serious relationships before they are ready or mature, it reduces the likelihood of success. Individuals shouldn't regard adult relationships like they're a junior high school crush or some college fling; they should be entered into soberly and prayerfully.

Several years ago, I was having a conversation with two single sisters, one who was in a serious relationship. After listening to them discussing relationships, I felt led to ask them what they thought marriage would be like. They responded with an idealistic fairytale fantasy that sounded like a Hollywood movie that included breakfast in bed every weekend, lengthy conversations over breakfast every morning, and quiet romantic dinners every night, not to mention several amazing vacations each year.

You can imagine their shock when I gave them a reality check after my laughter subsided. I told them that marriage is indeed wonderful but not because of those superficial reasons. Relationships are hard work, but when you get positive results, you realize it's worth the effort. I realized that many of our concepts and views of relationships and marriage are derived from movies, music, television, and now social media, with many naïve posts using the hashtag #relationshipgoals. Our upbringing at home and in the church can have a tremendous impact on how we view and approach relationships.

At one time in church culture, the tendency was to marry at a younger age than the general public. That was definitely the case for Carla and me; we got married when we were in our early twenties. Pastors and older church members encouraged and, in some cases, pushed young people to get married, often telling them, "It's better to marry than to burn." They didn't specify whether they were talking about burning with desire or burning in hell because of indulging in fornication; either way, they were more than eager to push young couples down the aisle. The problem was many of these young people weren't mature enough to handle the challenges of marriage. Sure, they were able to have guilt-free sex, but they weren't ready to communicate or work together to build a lasting relationship. They didn't realize all the work that was necessary to have a happy home and successful marriage.

Please don't think for one minute that I'm jaded or that I have a negative view of marriage. I'm a true believer in love and marriage especially when God brings two people together and their love blossoms and grows into a happy, long-lasting, loving relationship. I have been honored to officiate numerous wedding ceremonies, in my nearly thirty years of ministry, and I'm always hopeful and prayerful that it will last forever.

The ones that last have a few things in common:

1) Individually, they were mature adults and ready before they became a couple.

2) They were friends and enjoyed one another's company.

3) They each looked to make the other person happy; they submitted to one another.

4) They possessed an unselfish love and devotion to God and one another.

These aren't the only factors, but in my experience, they are four that stand out. Let's examine them individually.

Mature Adults Who Are Ready for a Mature Relationship Before They Become a Couple

Age isn't always the best or most accurate barometer of maturity. I've seen people that were in their early twenties that behaved with more maturity than individuals in their forties or fifties. I often tell young people not to even think about getting married until they're in their late twenties or early thirties because hopefully by that time, they should be a more fully developed young adult with a clear direction as it relates to their career and life. They also should have a better understanding of who they are. As the R&B songstress, Mary J. Blige sings in one of her early hits entitled Be Happy, "How can I love somebody else if I can't love myself?"

Before we jump into a relationship with another person, we need to know who we are, what our likes and dislikes are, where we are going, what we're bringing to the table, and the type of person we may be compatible with. We also need to have both moral and spiritual standards on which we shouldn't compromise. In addition to these qualities, each person must honestly assess where they are financially, mentally, physically, and emotionally. Major mistakes with long-lasting and sometimes dangerous consequences have been made when these factors are not taken into consideration. Now more than ever, men and women must be prayerful, careful, patient, and wise about who they get involved with. They must be sure both they and their potential spouse are mature and ready for a serious relationship.

One recent Saturday morning, Carla and I had the rare opportunity to sit down and talk to our two millennial children, Angela and Randall. They're both busy twenty-somethings, so it's not very often that we have a chance to talk as a family. This time we had a lively discussion about relationships, and in particular, how important maturity and patience are in making them last. My daughter voiced her frustration with how long it seems to take men to mature and decide to settle down. My son talked about how women don't always show their maturity either, especially on social media. They both agreed that many couples seem to be more focused on taking great pictures together for the public but aren't prepared to work on building a healthy relationship in real life. Some even go as far as having elaborate wedding ceremonies but aren't willing to work at having a happy marriage. We unanimously concluded that far too many young people (and quite a few old people) are not ready and lack the maturity to be in a serious relationship. Carla and I encouraged them by sharing our experiences as a couple that got married at a very young age and weathered the storms and ups and downs for over thirty-three years by God's grace. We told them that marriage is about growing with, adjusting to, and most of all loving one another enough to stick with each other, as you both continue to mature.

FRIENDS WHO ENJOY EACH OTHER'S COMPANY

One of the troubling aspects of many relationships these days is that some couples don't seem to enjoy one another's company; some don't even appear to be friends. With all of our modern conveniences—smartphones, tablets, laptops, and watches—we spend much of our time in a nearly constant state of distraction. We can put our earbuds in, close off everyone, and drift off into our own little world. It seems like many of us have difficulty having a conversation with the person right in front of us. The lack of verbal communication skills may be one of the factors in this generation's inability to build lasting friendships and thereby build healthy relationships.

Jesus says in the Gospel of John, "Greater love hath no man than this, that a man lay down his life for his friends" (John 15:13). Notice He didn't say marriage or a romantic relationship between a man and a woman was the greatest; He said friendship. He went on to tell His disciples that they were His friends—that their relationship had evolved from them being His servants to becoming His friends. As a relationship grows and evolves and the two individuals get to know one another by communicating, spending time with one another, and sharing experiences, then couples can truly become friends.

The bond of friendship is a tough one to break. Proverbs 17:17a says, "A friend loveth at all times . . ." When a married couple is having an argument, as every couple does, they will sometimes say something like this: "Don't do that to me, I'm your wife" or "How can you say that to me, I'm your husband?" We often place more emphasis on our positions or titles to make our spouse behave the way we'd like or treat us as they're supposed to. In reality, a better question would be, "How can you do that to me, I'm your friend?" or "How can you say that to me, I'm your friend?" Better still, couples should think to themselves I can't treat my friend like that, or I can't speak to my friend in that way. You never want to be the one that hurts your friend or causes your friend any pain.

Friends also enjoy spending time with one another. It doesn't have to be a special occasion or event. You just enjoy one another's company and you like being in each other's space. So many of the couples we see on social media seem to constantly be on the move or always around a large group of people. It makes you wonder if they ever spend time alone, just the two of them. Now, of course, they could be in very happy, strong marriages or have healthy, mature relationships, but I've also seen many of these public marriages end in divorce because away from the public, they had failed to cultivate a real friendship and didn't like one another's company. Mature relationships, where the individuals are friends first, don't seem to need a lot of extras. In fact, some of the best and most meaningful moments happen when you're not doing anything special except having a quiet conversation with the one you love—your best friend.

LOOKS TO MAKE THE OTHER PERSON HAPPY—SUBMITS TO EACH OTHER

Whenever I counsel couples, especially those that are soon to be married, I give them a homework assignment. They have to study Ephesians 5:21-32. The first verse of the passage says, "Submitting yourselves one to another in fear of God." Some of my old school male colleagues like to focus on the next verse which speaks about how wives should submit to their husbands as unto the Lord, but they stop short of verse twenty-five, that says a husband has to love his wife in the same way as Christ loved the church and gave Himself for it. The key verse that I want couples to take away from the study is verse twenty-one, because if couples submit to one another, if they're always seeking to make their spouse happy, then the verses that follow regarding submission, reverence, cleaving to one another, and even building a family, all have a greater chance of becoming more likely.

Submitting is a constant in a healthy, balanced marriage. It's important for both parties to give the other what they

need and try to make them happy. When one person in the relationship is always giving and the other is always taking, it's a
recipe for disaster. Selfish, self-centered people have a harder
time having successful relationships, especially when the other
person gets tired of always giving and never receiving anything
in return. It takes maturity to deal with the many challenges
every relationship faces, and couples need to be flexible and
willing to adjust to the changing circumstances. The chances of
success increase greatly when we are submitted to God and one
another. In our thirty-three years of marriage, Carla and I have
experienced many ups and downs, thankfully far more ups than
downs, and we've had to make many adjustments along the way,
but what sustains us is our love for God and one another. We
also maintain a desire to make each other happy by submitting
to one another, in the fear of the Lord.

Possesses an Unselfish Love and Devotion to God and One Another

Finally, the key to a lasting relationship is love. Love for God
and for one another First Corinthians 13 describes the attributes of charity or agape love, God's Love. It states that

> "Love is patient, love is kind. It does not envy, it does not
> boast, it is not proud. It does not dishonor others, it is not
> self-seeking, it is not easily angered, it keeps no record
> of wrongs. Love does not delight in evil but rejoices with
> the truth. It always protects, always trusts, always hopes,
> always perseveres. Love never fails." (1Corinthians 13:4-
> 8a NIV)

Whenever I read this passage, I realize how much more growth
and maturity is necessary for my own life and relationships.
Couples that strive to love like that not only have wonderful

relationships, but they can also build strong, loving families, and their children grow in a healthy, loving, and caring environment. It may not be perfect, but it's healthy.

So far, we have given great thought to mature marital relationships. Now, let's take a look at a biblical example of what a mature relationship looks like from the family dynamic.

The Lost Sons and the Father that Loved Them

Jesus had an interesting way of dealing with the criticisms of the scribes and Pharisees who were critical of the people who He ministered to and associated with. In Luke 15, He teaches a series of parables dealing with losing things of value and the response of those that found or recovered them. Each item increased in value (one out of 100 sheep, one out of 10 pieces of silver, one of two sons). Every time an item was found, the owners rejoiced and called others to celebrate with them. Jesus compared the celebrations to the joy in heaven over one soul that repents.

The last parable deals with two sons, the younger of which asks his father for his portion of his inheritance early, an act that was tantamount to saying, "I wish you were dead." He showed disrespect and immaturity by saying, "Give me the portion of goods that falleth to me." Immature, childish people underestimate the value of people and relationships and often place too high a value on material things. Like spoiled children, they simply want immediate gratification.

The father gives BOTH sons their portions early. Sometimes individuals are gifted, but they are too immature to handle it properly. Others are gifted with blessings they did not ask for and do not appreciate. The younger son demonstrates his immaturity by taking his inheritance to a far country and wasting it on riotous, reckless living, spending money, time, and energy behaving in a way that only brings temporary joy that does not last.

The Lord's mercy and grace cover us until we come to ourselves, have a moment of clarity, and realize we can do better. We understand that we are not supposed to be here. The younger son began to grow up in the hog pen when he saw who he had become, remembered who he was supposed to be, and who his father was. Maturity is when you are able to look at yourself honestly (as you really are) and view your sin the same way God does; this leads to confession and repentance. He went from being a spoiled and entitled brat to being willing to be a humble servant, ready to work for what he got. He may have been weak, hungry, and tired, but he stayed focused on getting back to his father's house, so he could repent and confess.

Clearly, the star of the parable is the father who is looking for and expecting the immature, wayward son to come home. He sees him afar off, has compassion on him, and runs to him hugging and kissing him, demonstrating how we are to receive our "wayward" sons and daughters into the Kingdom. The prodigal son is restored to his place in the family with his ring, sandals, and his robe, symbolizing his being covered once again. The father calls for a great celebration to commence because his son was lost, but now is found; he was dead, but now is alive. He is mature in his relationship as a father, not treating the son with disdain or disgust.

However, the immaturity of the elder son is exposed by his reaction to the news that his brother was home and they were having a party. We can measure our maturity by how we react when someone else is blessed or is restored. When you grow up, you can celebrate even when it is not your turn. The oldest son pouts and throws a tantrum, criticizing his brother and pointing out all of his sins. Once again, the father goes out to his son and shows love and patience with his immature son.

How much better would our ministries, families, and communities be if we learned how to have love, compassion, and patience with immature, wayward sons and daughters? Those of us that are leaders must learn to do what the apostle Paul advised in 2 Timothy 2:24-26:

> "And the servant of the Lord must not strive; but be gentle unto all men, apt to teach, patient, In meekness instructing those that oppose themselves; if God peradventure will give them repentance to the acknowledging of the truth; And that they may recover themselves out of the snare of the devil, who are taken captive by him at his will."

It is important for pastors and leaders to grow and mature along with their members. Not many of us would have handled our sons the way the prodigal's father did. I'm sure we all have fascinating stories about "difficult" church members. We're human and we hurt as well. But if we're truly honest, we all have had moments where we mishandled situations and people, and we dealt with them in immature ways. I can think of several instances in my pastoral career, as a parent, and husband, where I did not handle situations with the right level of grace, maturity, or patience that was required.

I remember an incident several years ago where a member and I ended up shouting at each other over the phone, and I was sure that we would not ever speak to or see each other again. But thank God for grace, mercy, and maturity! Both of us had to admit that we were wrong. Sometimes pastors have a hard time admitting that they were wrong and apologizing. But, many times, our prayers are hindered, and our blessings are held up because of unforgiveness, bitterness, and holding grudges. We must release all that stuff, become like the prodigal son's father and love our members with the love that the Lord has shown us. Because we chose to press forward differently, I am elated to say that former member and I have a wonderful relationship now, thanks to God's love and the fact that we both have grown and matured.

Chapter 9

Mature Mind Attributes:
Surrendering My Mind to Christ

*M*any of you are probably asking yourselves, "What now? How do I finally get to a place of spiritual maturity?" or "Are there some practical steps I can take to become the person God has called me to be?" Of course, the answer to these questions is a resounding YES! There are steps we all must take to reach maturity. Let's focus on four important areas that will help us increase our capacity for more and accelerate the maturation process:

1. **Identify**: The first step we must take is to find out who we are in Christ. We also need to identify the gifts and talents He has given us. Prayer and spiritual counseling as well as conversations with people you trust can be beneficial in this process.

2. **Recognize**: We need to recognize where we are. We have to be honest with ourselves and examine our level of growth, while acknowledging shortcomings as well as strengths.

3. **Discover**: It's critical that we discover our purpose. Why does the Lord have me here? What are His plans for my life? What things are hindering me from walking in my purpose? Again, time in prayer, the Word of God, and spiritual counseling will help in this area.

4. **Navigate**: Now we can chart our course to our destiny. Once we've taken the first three steps, then the Lord can give us more because now we're focused on where He wants us to go.

It is critical that we seek God's face and hear His assessment of where we are spiritually. We must spend time alone with Him, in prayer and consecration, turning off all noise and eliminating all distractions to hear His still small voice. Our ability to remain focused will be tested, especially when you've made up your mind to fulfill your purpose. There may come a time when we'll need to make a completely honest assessment of ourselves and come to grips with how and why we got off track. It's like when we are driving to an unfamiliar destination and we have the GPS programmed and it's giving us directions. It's important that we pay attention and not get so wrapped up in conversation with other passengers or with someone on the phone, that we miss the next instruction and cause the GPS to recalculate our course and we further delay our arrival. When we lose focus and get off track or make a wrong turn because we didn't hear God's voice, we need to eliminate the distractions, make a U-turn and get back on course. That's the time to simplify our lives, get back to prayer and reading the Word, as well as having meaningful conversations with people that support you and hold you accountable.

Finally, it comes down to these three:

1) Do I really want to change, or am I satisfied with my life just the way it is?

2) Can I be better? Do I want to be better?

3) Am I living my best life, my God-ordained life?

Romans 12:1 admonishes us to present our bodies as a living sacrifice. If we want our lives to change and to be transformed, we must release our life into God's hands. Yielding to Him positions us for transformation. When we surrender ourselves to Him completely, then our minds can be renewed, and our lives transformed. Whatever part of us that we do not yield to Him cannot be changed. There are some things that we cannot hold on to and go to the next level. This giving of ourselves to God is our "logical, intelligent act of worship." (Roman12:1, AMP) "And be not conformed to this world: but be ye transformed by the renewing of your mind." (Romans 12:2)

We cannot fully mature and our lives cannot change until our minds are renewed. We must think differently if we are going to speak differently and walk differently. Mind renewal is an ongoing process where our old way of thinking, conforming to the latest fad, or fleeting behaviors of society, is replaced by a new way of thinking: focusing on godly values and ethical attitudes. Metamorphosis is from the inside out, like a caterpillar becoming a butterfly. Others may not be able to see what is going on inside your cocoon, but a brand new you will soon emerge, operating on a different level.

A renewed mind is vital to the spiritual growth and maturity of the believer. Paul wrote to the Roman believer, "but be transformed and progressively changed [as you mature spiritually] by the renewal of your mind." (Romans 12:2a, AMP) When we mature, the will of God becomes clearer and we find out that His divine plan and purpose for our lives is "so that you may prove [for yourselves] what the will of God is, that which is good and acceptable and perfect [in his plan and purpose for you]." (Romans 12:2b, AMP)

How do you know when you are becoming spiritually mature and beginning to grow? What does spiritual maturity look like? In Matthew 12:33, Jesus says, "A tree is known by its fruit," describing how our words reveal our true character. Our spiritual fruitfulness also tells us how much we have matured. This is one way we can measure our growth.

In Galatians 5, Paul writes to the church to encourage them concerning spiritual liberty. He encourages them to "walk in the Spirit" and not "fulfill the lusts of the flesh." (Galatians 5:16) He talked about the battle between the flesh and the Spirit, and in doing so described the "works of the flesh" and the "fruit of the Spirit." When we are immature, we find our behavior will exhibit some of the following characteristics: carnality, sexually immorality, idolatry and witchcraft, hatred, discord, jealousy, fits of rage, tantrums, selfish ambition, total irresponsibility, lack of self-control, disputes, envy, drunkenness, riotous behavior, etc. We find ourselves repeating the same vicious cycles over and over again which hinder us from getting on track and moving to the next level.

But when Paul describes the fruit of the Spirit, it is here that we can begin to measure our growth and level of maturity. He says, "But the fruit of the Spirit (the result of His presence with us) is love (unselfish concern for others), joy, (inner) peace, patience (not the ability to wait, but how we act while waiting), kindness, goodness, faithfulness, gentleness, and self-control." (Galatians 5:22-23 AMP)

When you have a mature mind and when your behavior and attitude changes, you will not have to apologize or ask for forgiveness as often because you will not offend and upset as many people. You will not be as confrontational. People will know you are mature, not by what you say, but by the fruit of the Spirit that is evident in your everyday life. You will be able to see it, too, when you are believing differently in situations and where you used to go off or lose it, you now find yourself calm, cool, and collected.

It is critical for believers to have the fruit of the Spirit flourishing and becoming more evident in our everyday lives, so that we can have a greater impact on our families, jobs, churches, and communities.

But why does it seem that some of us get to certain places or make progress in a particular area, but fail to experience the breakthrough that God has shown us was ours? I believe one of the hindrances is our inability to focus. One sign of immaturity is when an individual is easily distracted and unable to pay attention for extended periods of time or unable to focus on the task at hand.

I remember when I was a junior in high school taking an honors Geometry class that had quite a few very pretty girls in it. The girls captured my attention, and much to my surprise, I seemed to have theirs as well. They actually engaged in conversation with me and even laughed at my silly antics. Once I found out I could make them laugh, that became my focus for the entire semester. Of course, I wasn't paying any attention to the teacher's lessons and kept falling further and further behind.

The D I received on the midterm shocked me, but the F I received as a final grade shook me to my core. I learned a very valuable lesson that by behaving in an immature manner and playing around, I had lost focus and gotten completely off track. I had forgotten who I was and my purpose for being in school. The material wasn't too difficult; it was my immaturity that allowed me to become distracted. I had failed to apply myself to my lessons and had to suffer the consequences of my actions. I ended up transferring from that school. I retook Geometry and received an A. I learned a valuable lesson that I still carry with me today; don't allow yourself to be easily distracted from your assignment but give your all to the task that's in front of you.

As believers, if we want to be transformed into the people God has called us to be, we must give ourselves completely to Him and remain focused, no matter what! We can't allow people or circumstances to distract us or get us off track. God will transform us from the inside out, then we can recognize what His will is for our lives and fulfill our destiny. Society will try to keep dragging us down to its level of immaturity and foolishness, but God will bring out the best in us and develop well-formed maturity in each one of us.

Chapter 10

Mature Living:
Disciples Produce Much Fruit

*Y*ou were created by God to be fruitful. Adam and Eve were instructed to be fruitful and multiply. Noah and his sons were told the same thing after the flood. Finally, Jesus instructed His disciples in John 15 that they were branches and He was the True Vine. He said if a branch did not produce, it would be taken away, and if it did produce (or bring forth fruit), it would be pruned to produce more fruit. One of the challenges of growth and maturity is how we handle the pruning process. When the Lord begins to cut some things, habits, or even people out of our lives, it hurts. When this happens to us for the first time, it is so painful that we wonder if we can ever recover.

When the Lord began to move people out of the ministry after we had experienced significant growth, I was extremely upset and confused. I wondered had I done something wrong and why would God let this happen. I did not understand that the reason we had to cut some people and things out of my life/ministry was because it was growing, and I was maturing. He was doing it so that I would bring forth "more fruit." One of the signs of growth and maturity is not just how much fruit you are producing, but how do you handle the pruning process. How do we deal with growing pains when your ministry, business, or position on your job changes? How do we respond to the Lord working on certain aspects of our character and behavior that hinder our growth? Jesus said,

> "You have not chosen Me, but I have chosen you and I have appointed, placed and purposefully planted you so that you would go and bear fruit and keep on bearing, and that your fruit will remain and be lasting, so that whatever you ask the Father in my name [as My representative] He may give to you. (John 15:16 AMP)

That is a level of growth and maturity that we all should be aiming for. We must realize that when the Lord is pruning us, He is really preparing us to bring forth much fruit.

As I mentioned earlier, the Lord has called us to advance His kingdom in the earth. Not only do we do that by using the keys that He has given to us, but we also do it by living mature lives.

When Jesus began His earthly ministry with the multitudes following Him, He taught a series of lessons which became The Sermon on the Mount. In Matthew 5:1-11, we find the first message commonly known as The Beatitudes or Blessings, which laid out a pathway of spiritual growth and showed believers what a mature, kingdom lifestyle looked like. He taught us how we can grow in grace and knowledge and have favor with God and our fellow man.

If you ask most Christians for a definition of what it means to be blessed, they would probably give you a list of material things: houses, cars, clothes, money, or they may mention their career, social status, or even their physical attributes. The blessedness that Jesus is referring to in Matthew has nothing to do with material, tangible possessions. It doesn't even refer to favorable circumstances in life. This blessedness comes from the inside out. When the Lord is transforming your life and you begin to grow spiritually, you understand that material things come and go and circumstances change, but you can still consider yourself blessed, even if you don't have everything you want.

One important thing that must be understood in relation to the Beatitudes is the blessedness described in them is not static or all on the same level, but it is progressive. Our progress depends on the fulfillment of the conditions laid out on each level of these beatitudes.

This state of blessedness begins the moment a person believes on Jesus Christ for salvation. When we start living according to these principles, we position ourselves on a pathway of continual growth and elevation. Each one of these beatitudes represent another rung on the ladder that leads to a mature life.

The first step is humility: "Blessed are the poor in spirit: for theirs is the kingdom of heaven." (Matthew 5:3) The amplified translation describes the "poor in spirit" as "those devoid of spiritual arrogance and those who regard themselves as insignificant." When we are humble and continue to acknowledge that we need God and can't live without Him, He gives us the Kingdom of heaven. Humility is essential for spiritual growth and development.

When The Lord says, "Blessed are they that mourn: for they shall be comforted" (Matthew 5:4), He's not talking about grieving for someone that has passed away, but He's referring to mourning our sins and the sins of others. The blessedness is that we're forgiven and we're comforted when the burden of sin and guilt is lifted.

We usually associate meekness with weakness, but actually meekness is having great inner strength and is an indication of spiritual maturity. "Blessed are the meek: for they shall inherit the earth." (Matthew 5:5) First you see yourself as you really are in relation to God, and therefore see others in a more realistic light. Meekness is an inner grace of soul that enables us to accept God's dealings with us as good, without resistance or reservation. Aristotle described meekness as, "The middle course in being angry, standing between two extremes, getting angry without reason and not getting angry at all." It means getting angry at the right time, in the right measure, for the right reason. You can tell you have matured when the people and situations that used to set you off in the past, no longer affect you the same way.

"Blessed are they which do hunger and thirst after righteousness: for they shall be filled." (Matthew 5:6) As we mature, our appetite for the things of God will increase. Our appetite for His presence, His Word, and to hear His voice will become constant and reoccurring. Once we've been satisfied, the desire for more will return. The more we get, the more we'll want.

How we treat others will also change as we grow and develop. "Blessed are the merciful: for they shall obtain mercy." (Matthew 5:7) It takes maturity to forgive others and release those that have done us wrong. It becomes easier when we consider how merciful the Lord has been to us. I can't hold anything against you because I don't want Jesus to hold any of my sins against me.

By the time we get to, "Blessed are the pure in heart: for they shall see God" (Matthew 5:8), we have reached a level where God continuously cleanses us because we have fulfilled the previous conditions of blessedness. As it says in the amplified translation, "Blessed [anticipating God's presence, spiritually mature] are the pure in heart . . ." The purer we become, the clearer God becomes; the clearer He becomes, the purer He makes us.

The peacemakers are not just people who try to resolve conflicts between individuals. Matthew 5:9 states, "Blessed are the peacemakers: for they shall be called the children of God." We have the peace of God guarding our hearts and minds and we bring that peace into every situation, because it's with us all the time.

Imagine being so mature and living your life at a level where you're so connected to God that when people persecute you and speak all manner of evil against you, that you can rejoice in all types of situations and circumstances. "Blessed are ye when men shall revile you and persecute you and say all manner of evil against you . . ." "Rejoice and be exceedingly glad: for great is your reward in heaven . . ." (Matthew 5:11-12)

Jesus calls those that have reached this level of blessedness; "the salt of the earth" and "the light of the world"; in other words, we should be a preservative and seasoning, as well as bringing illumination to a dark world. When we mature, we should have an impact on everyone we come in contact with.

My prayer for each one of us is that we continue to grow, develop, and mature into the men and women that God has called us to be. May the Lord release the full measure of His Grace and Power upon us, as we manifest His Divine Will for our lives.

About the Author

Stephen Hamilton is a dynamic teacher, preacher and leader of Spirit and Life Ministries, Inc. (SLM).

Born in 1963, baptized in 1969, and filled with the Holy Ghost at he ripe young age of 11, Pastor Hamilton not only comes from a family dedicated to worshiping the Lord, but he has dedicated his life to it. In 1987, Pastor Hamilton began attending Aenon Bible College, was ordained in 1990, began preaching in 1986, and became a Pastor in 1991. Under the leadership of Bishop Robert T. Douglas, Sr., on January 16, 2015, Pastor Hamilton was installed as a District Elder within the Central California District Council under the Pentecostal Assemblies of the World, Inc. A short time later, on July 15, 2016, he elevated to Suffragan Bishop at the CCDC Summer 2016 Conference.

Since he was called to the ministry, he has dedicated his life to empowering individuals, organizations, and a growing multicultural congregation towards changing the world. His ministry of reconciliation has inspired men, women and young people nationwide for decades.

This anointed leader delivers the Word of God with power, simplicity, and humor that intensifies the relevancy of his message to the everyday person. In 2006, Pastor Hamilton established the Spirit and Life Institute, a full-service institution that converges practical life experiences with faith-based teaching to develop well-rounded Christians that live in abundance...now!

A friend to all from government officials, power brokers, and celebrities to the blue-collar worker, college student and stay-at-home parent, Pastor Hamilton moves amongst society while connecting the gospel of Jesus Christ and its practical implementation to maximize the daily living experience.

Based in the San Fernando Valley, Pastor Hamilton is a frequent guest preacher, teacher, and speaker at churches across the country. He has also appeared in various shows, documentaries, and networks, such as BET (Black Entertainment Television) and TV One.

Pastor Hamilton has received numerous awards and commendations from Los Angeles County Supervisor Michael D. Antonovich, Los Angeles Councilman Tony Cardenas, California State Senator Alex Padilla, former Los Angeles Police Department Chief Bernard Parks, and U.S. Councilwoman Maxine Waters, and many others that have recognized his diligent work in the ministry.

Under his leadership, Spirit and Life Ministries was also awarded the Steve Harvey Morning Show's "Hoodie Award*" for "Best Church in Los Angeles."

A resident of the East Valley since childhood, Pastor Hamilton shares his life with his beautiful wife, First Lady Carla Hamilton, and their son and daughter.

To contact Stephen Hamilton for speaking engagements, book signings or tours,

BWilson.SHMinistries@gmail.com
12962 Vaughn Street San Fernando, CA 91340
818-896-5022
www.SteveHamiltonMinistries.com

Connect with Bishop Hamilton
Twitter: @stevehamilton50
Instagram: @stephenh_50
Facebook: @bishopshm